Diet recommendations for acute pancreatitis

Please check these recommendations always with a nutrition
consultant, therapist, doctor or dietician. The recipes and the list of
ingredients are supporting the conventional medical therapy.
The calorie disclosures of fresh ingredients (fruit and vegetables) vary
according to quality and time of harvest. The contents were checked by
a dietician and a nutrition consultant for the Traditional Chinese
Medicine (TCM).

Author:
©2017 Josef Miligui
www.ebns.at

AF199921

Source:
The lists are created from the EBNS database for nutritional counseling.
The database is used by dietitians, therapists and doctors for advising
the patient / client.

Literature:
The specialist literature and the training documents of the German and
Austrian dietary and traditional Chinese medicine serve as a knowledge
base. We have used the documents as a basis of knowledge, adapted it
to our experience and completed them.
http://di-book.com

Title Photo:
©2008 Erika Weixlbaumer

Production and publishing:
BoD – Books on Demand, Norderstedt
ISBN 9783746026008

Diet recommendations for DIETETICS - Gastrointestinal tract - Pancreas - Acute pancreatitis (inflammation of the pancreas)

1 Treatment strategy

Step 1 (according to medical prescription):
Nutritional benefit: no oral nutrient and fluid intake
Stage 2 (Day 1):

Carbohydrates: sweetened tea, rusk, mucus soup
Stage 3 (2nd to 4th day):
Low fat protein: skimmed milk products, white bread, meat and fish (low fat)
Step 4 (5th - 7th day):
High-fiber foods, potatoes, vegetables, larger portions
Step 5 (8-15 days):
Fat in small portions: cheese (low fat), egg, meat and fish
Step 6 (16 - 21 day):
Light normal diet: finely ground whole grain products, no raw food, no flourishing vegetables and legumes;
 6 - 8 small meals, which should be carefully prepared: cooking and steaming, low-fat frying.
After the symptoms have subsided, a light meal or normal diet is usually prescribed.

2 Avoid

Alcohol, fat food.

3 Breakfast

4 Snack

5 Lunch

6 Afternoon

7 Dinner

8 Any time

9 Recipes

(recommendable) = You can use more.
(little) = You should use less than specified or omit.

9.1 Asparagus Cream Soup

Diuretic, improves blood circulation, prevents cancer, laxative, antiparasitic, stimulates liver function, good to fight loss of appetite, flatulence, rheumatism, heartburn.
Cooking time approx. 45 min
Calories p. portion: 240
2 portions
Allergens: ACG

Quantity of ingredients:
Parsley 2 table spoons / 20g. (recommended)
Asparagus (green or white) 5/8 oz / 200g. (recommended)
Water 2 cup / 500g. (yes)
Rapeseed oil 2 table spoons / 30g. (little)
Wheat flour 2 table spoons / 10g. (yes)
Chicken yolk 1 piece / 25g. (little)
Cow's milk (whole milk 3.5% fat) 1 table spoon / 15g. (yes)
Sour cream 15% fat 1 table spoon / 15g. (little)
Pepper (ground) 1 pinch / 0,5g. (little)
Lemon juice 1 teaspoon / 2g. ()
Salt 1 pinch / 1g. (little)
Nutmeg 1 pinch / 0,5g. (recommended)

Cooking instructions:
Wash and peel the asparagus.
Heat water, a little lemon juice and pinch of salt till it boils. Tie the asparagus spears together.
Add the asparagus peel to the cooking water and bring to the boil.
Add the asparagus and cook on low heat for about 20 minutes.
Then remove the asparagus bunches and pour the broth through a sieve.
For the roux, heat the oil in a saucepan, add the flour and sauté until it is colorless, slowly top up with the asparagus sauce and simmer for 10 minutes.
Cut the asparagus spears into pieces about 3 cm long and place them to the soup.
Just before serving, bring the soup to boil again.
Mix the egg yolk with the milk and sour cream.

Remove the pot from the heat and stir in the egg yolk and milk mixture. Season with pepper and nutmeg, decorate with the chopped parsley and serve immediately.

9.2   Baked chicory

Mineral supporter and is full of A-B-C vitamins.
Cooking time approx. 20 min
Calories p. portion: 230
2 portions
Allergens: AG

Quantity of ingredients:
Cream, sweet 30% 2 table spoons / 40g. ()
Breadcrumbs (wheat bread, bread roll) 2 table spoons / 20g. (yes)
Salt 1 pinch / 1g. (little)
Water 3 cups / 300g. (yes)
Rice Basmati 1/2 cup / 60g. (yes)
Chicory 4 pieces / 500g. (yes)

Cooking instructions:
Blanch chicory in hot water whole for about 5 minutes; place in a casserole dish; put some sweet cream over it; put the bread crumbs over the chicory and gratinate.

Place the rice in salted water, heat till it boils and let it simmer over low heat for about 15 minutes.

9.3   Barley mash with berries

Diuretic, forcing spleen, supports urination, laxative, strengthens kidney, promotes digestion, detoxifying, promotes perspiration, reduces blood lipids, stimulates, dissolves stagnation.
Cooking time approx. 2 hours
Calories p. portion: 113
5 portions
Allergens: A

Quantity of ingredients:
Barley malt 1 table spoon / 15g. (yes)
Salt 1 pinch / 1g. (little)
Cocoa 1 pinch / 1g. (yes)
Raspberry 5/8 lbs - 8oz / 250g. (recommended)
Barley 1 cup / 120g. (yes)
Water 10 cups / 1200g. (yes)
Cardamom 3 capsules / 1g. (recommended)
Ginger fresh 2 slices / 2g. (recommended)
Lemon Balm (fresh) 2-4 leaves / 3g. (yes)

Cooking instructions:
Boil the barley with water, ginger and cardamom pods in a large
saucepan. Close pot with a lid and cook over low heat for about 2
hours.

For 2 servings of cooked barley porridge, place about 2 ladles in a bowl.
Stir with sunflower seeds, malt, cocoa powder and a pinch of salt. Stir
fresh berries into the porridge and serve sprinkled with fresh mint or
lemon balm.

Tip: The pre-cooked barley porridge (without fruit) can be stored well in
the refrigerator and used for sweet or savory dishes, e.g. with stewed
vegetables or fruit seasoned compote.

9.4   Barley soup

Diuretic, forcing spleen, supports urination, stimulates liver function,
antioxidativ, promotes digestion, detoxifying, reduces blood lipids,
stimulates, dissolves stagnation.
Cooking time approx. 25 min
Calories p. portion: 265
2 portions
Allergens: A

Quantity of ingredients:
Parsley 2 table spoons / 30g. (recommended)
Ginger fresh 1/2 teaspoon / 1g. (recommended)
Barley 1 cup / 120g. (yes)
Olive oil 1 table spoon / 10g. (little)
Water 1 1/2 cups / 240g. (yes)
Salt 1 pinch / 1g. (little)

Cooking instructions:
Roast the barley in the pan, then grind it to the ground, and boil with water, some salt and ginger to a mash. Before serving add oil and parsley.
Variant: You can add a better taste to the dish if you cook it with prepared vegetable or meat broth.

9.5   Basic recipe for a reissue soup (Congee)

Low fat content, for the drainage of the body overweight and high blood pressure.
Cooking time approx. 2-4 hours
Calories p. portion: 140
3 portions
Allergens:

Quantity of ingredients:
Water 6 cups / 700g. (yes)
Rice variety any 1 cup / 120g. (yes)

Cooking instructions:
Cook rice and water in a ratio of about 1: 6. The amount of water determines the thickness of the mash (matter of taste).
Put the rice in a saucepan with a heavy lid. It is important to simmer the rice after a short boil on the slightest flame, otherwise it burns.
Boil the rice for 2-4 hours. The longer he cooks, the more he strengthens.
If you want to eat the dish for breakfast, you can put the rice on just before bedtime.
To be on the safe side, you should first check the behavior of your pot and cooker under observation for a similar amount of time, so that nothing burns.
Refrigerate for later use.

9.6   Basic recipe for a vegetable soup, nutritious

Reduces blood pressure, strengthens immune system, prevents cancer, forcing spleen, dissolves stagnation, promotes weight loss. Good to fight immunodeficiency, high blood pressure, depressions, diabetes, diarrhea, reduces blood lipids.
Cooking time approx. 2-3 hours
Calories p. portion: 48
5 portions
Allergens: L

Quantity of ingredients:
Salt 1 pinch / 1g. (little)
Thyme dried 1 pinch / 1g. (yes)
Lovage 1 table spoon / 3g. (recommended)
Bay leaf 2 leaves / 1g. (recommended)
Olive oil 1 table spoon / 4g. (little)
Ginger fresh 1/2 teaspoon / 2g. (recommended)
Juniper berry 6 pieces / 6g. (recommended)
Celery root 1 cup / 100g. (recommended)
Lemon 1/2 piece / 25g. ()
Parsnip 3/8 lbs - 6oz / 150g. (recommended)
Carrot 3 pieces / 200g. (recommended)
Water 3 cups / 650g. (yes)
Onion white 1 piece / 60g. ()

Cooking instructions:
Cut the vegetables into cubes.
Heat oil in hot pot, fry shortly onions and vegetables.
Add cold water, then add ginger, bay leaf and lemon juice.
Season with juniper, thyme and lovage. Cover for 2 - 3 hours on a low heat and simmer.
The used vegetables should be thrown away.
The basic recipe serves as a soup base and to refine vegetables, legumes or cereals.
If you want to eat vegetable soup immediately, add the desired vegetables half an hour before.
Refrigerate for later use.

9.7   Black root with yogurt

Stimulates kidney, bladder and forces the cleaning of the body. In the physiological sense, they generally stimulate the glands in the organism. Good to fight acute or chronic constipation of the intestine. Rich in Vitamins and trace elements.
Cooking time approx. 20 min
Calories p. portion: 424
2 portions
Allergens: AG

Quantity of ingredients:
Salt 1 pinch / 1g. (little)
Herbs various 1 table spoon / 8g. (yes)
Herbs various 2 table spoons / 6g. (yes)
Yogurt (natural, 1.5% fat) 4 table spoons / 80g. (recommended)
Multi-grain bread (gray bread) 6 slices / 120g. (little)
Salsify 1 lbs / 400g. (recommended)

Cooking instructions:
Peel the salsify and simmer in salted water until tender. Pour away the water, cool the salsify and cut it to size.
Cover with yoghurt and sprinkle with fresh herbs. Serve with the bread. You can also use the salsify from the conserve.

9.8   Blueberry puree

Bilberry is laxative. Clove dissolves stagnation. Cinnamon powder heats stomach and spleen, improves blood circulation.
Cooking time approx. 10 min
Calories p. portion: 10
1 portions
Allergens:

Quantity of ingredients:
Blueberry 1/2 oz / 20g. (recommended)
Clove 1 piece / 1g. (recommended)
Water 1 cup / 250g. (yes)
Cinnamon ground 1 pinch / 0,1g. (recommended)

Cooking instructions:
Boil blueberries with cinnamon and clove in water for 10 minutes.
Remove the cinnamon and clove. Puree. Sweet as desired.

9.9   Carrot and rice gruel soup

Stops diarrhea, good to fight fever, strengthens immune system, reduces blood pressure.
Cooking time approx. 10 min
Calories p. portion: 101
1 portions
Allergens:

Quantity of ingredients:
Carrot 2 pieces / 100g. (recommended)
Basic recipe for a rice soup (Congee) 1 cup / 120g. (recommended)
Salt 1 teaspoon / 4g. (little)

Cooking instructions:
Peel and grate carrots. Heat the rice soup (according to the basic recipe) till it boils and add the grated carrots and salt. Cook for 10 minutes.

9.10 Compote from apples

Apple (sweet) stops diarrhea, promotes digestion, appetizing, harmonizes the stomach, improves blood circulation.
Cooking time approx. 10 min
Calories p. portion: 67
2 portions
Allergens:

Quantity of ingredients:
Water 1 1/2 cups / 220g. (yes)
Cinnamon ground 1 pinch / 1g. (recommended)
Apple (sweet) 1 piece / 220g. (yes)

Cooking instructions:
Cook the apples (organic) with the skin and seeds. Sprinkle with cinnamon.

9.11 Compote from rhubarb

Antipyretic, analgesic, detoxifying, bactericide.
Cooking time approx. 15 min
Calories p. portion: 48
1 portions
Allergens:

Quantity of ingredients:
Water 1 cup / 120g. (yes)
Honey 1 table spoon / 10g. (recommended)
Rhubarb 1/4 lbs - 4oz / 100g. (recommended)

Cooking instructions:
Wash rhubarb and cut small. Boil in the water. Allow to cool a little and add the honey.

9.12 Corn coffee with cardamom

Diuretic, forcing spleen, supports urination, relaxes, reduces fat.
Cooking time approx. 5 min
Calories p. portion: 3
1 portions
Allergens:

Quantity of ingredients:
Cereal coffee 1 table spoon / 15g. (yes)
Cardamom 2 cores / 1g. (recommended)
Water 1 cup / 120g. (yes)

Cooking instructions:
Boil water, coffee, sugar and cardamom. Let it set for one min before drinking.

9.13 Cranberry juice

Antibacterial, good to fight loss of appetite, arteriosclerosis, bladder infections, diarrhea, colds. Antipyretic, against free radicals, gout, diuretic, stomach ulcers, oral mucosa inflammation, rheumatism.
Cooking time approx. 5 min
Calories p. portion: 43
1 portions
Allergens:

Quantity of ingredients:
Honey 1 table spoon / 10g. (recommended)
Water 1 cup / 125g. (yes)
Cranberries 2 table spoons / 25g. (yes)

Cooking instructions:
Mix the cranberries with a little water with the blender to a pulp. Add the remaining water and sweeten with the honey.

9.14 Cranberry yogurt mix

Good to fight acute or chronic constipation of the intestine, oral mucosal inflammation, diarrhea, flatulence, throat irritation.
Cooking time approx. 5 min
Calories p. portion: 57
2 portions
Allergens: GO

Quantity of ingredients:
Mineral water 1 cup / 250g. (little)
Cranberry jam 2 table spoons / 20g. (yes)
Yogurt (natural, 1.5% fat) 1/4 lbs - 4oz / 125g. (recommended)

Cooking instructions:
Mix yoghurt, cranberry jam and mineral water until frothy.

9.15 Fried asparagus with rocket

Diuretic, improves blood circulation, prevents cancer, stimulates digestion, forcing spleen, promotes weight loss. Good to fight immunodeficiency, loss of appetite, arteriosclerosis, flatulence, bladder weakness, anemia, high blood pressure, depressions, diabetes.
Cooking time approx. 15 min
Calories p. portion: 149
3 portions
Allergens: G

Quantity of ingredients:
Salt 1 pinch / 1g. (little)
Pepper (ground) 1 pinch / 0,5g. (little)
Butter Bio 1 table spoon / 20g. (little)
Potato 3/4 lbs / 300g. (recommended)
Rucola 2 handful / 30g. (recommended)
Asparagus (green or white) 1,1 lbs / 500g. (recommended)
Lemon 1/4 piece / 12g. ()

Cooking instructions:
Melt a piece of butter in a hot pan; cut the peeled asparagus into pieces of 3 to 4 cm, fry for about 10 minutes until
tender, but crisp. Sprinkle with freshly ground pepper, salt, add a few drops of lemon juice or finely grated lemon
zest, finely shredded rucola leaves.
Cook the potatoes in plenty of salted water, then peel.

9.16 Frozen pineapple juice

Pineapple reduce inflammation, supports urination, cleans the skin.
Cooking time approx. 1 1/2 hours
Calories p. portion: 29
1 portions
Allergens:

Quantity of ingredients:
Pineapple 1/8 lbs - 2oz / 50g. (yes)

Cooking instructions:
Juice pineapple yourself or freeze the organic pineapple juice in small portions and if necessary suck.

9.17 Fruit juice

Stops diarrhea, promotes digestion, appetizing, harmonizes the stomach, relieves pain, detoxifying, reduces blood pressure, strengthens immune system, prevents cancer, reduces radiation damage.
Cooking time approx. 10 min
Calories p. portion: 176
2 portions
Allergens:

Quantity of ingredients:
Honey 1 table spoon / 10g. (recommended)
Carrot 2 pieces / 150g. (recommended)
Apple (sweet) 4 pieces / 300g. (yes)
Orange 2 pieces / 150g. (yes)

Cooking instructions:
Peel oranges and carrots. Cut all ingredients into cubes so that they fit into the juicer and juice. Sweet with honey.

9.18 Grated apple

Eat 3 times a day - Apple (sour) scraped and brown is stuffing. Relieves diarrhea.
Cooking time approx. 10 min
Calories p. portion: 120
1 portions
Allergens:

Quantity of ingredients:
Apple (sour) 1 piece / 200g. (yes)

Cooking instructions:
Peel apple and grate as fine as possible. Leave for at least 5 minutes until it turns brown.

9.19 Mango banana yoghurt drink ice cold

Good to fight loss of appetite, oral mucosa inflammation. Regulates gastrointestinal function, chronic constipation. Prevents cancer. Diuretic, forcing spleen.
Cooking time approx. 5 min
Calories p. portion: 121
2 portions
Allergens: G

Quantity of ingredients:
Banana 1/2 piece / 150g. (yes)
Mango juice 1/2 cup / 100g. (yes)
Mineral water 1/2 cup / 100g. (little)
Yogurt (natural, 1.5% fat) 1/4 lbs - 4oz / 100g. (recommended)
Acerola fruit nectar or powder 1 teaspoon / 2g. (yes)

Cooking instructions:
Mix all the ingredients and 2-3 ice cubes in a blender.

9.20 Nettle-chard soup

Nettle promotes urination, detoxifies, supporting prostate disorders, reduces inflammation, analgesic. Chard supports intestinal activity, cleans intestine.
Cooking time approx. 30 min
Calories p. portion: 52
4 portions
Allergens:

Quantity of ingredients:
Water 2 cup / 400g. (yes)
Olive oil 1 table spoon / 10g. (little)
Salt 1 pinch / 1g. (little)
Nettles Handful / 10g. (yes)
Pepper (ground) 1 pinch / 0,5g. (little)
Chard 1 lbs / 500g. (recommended)

Cooking instructions:
Heat the oil in a saucepan, add the washed and finely chopped Swiss chard. Salt and let simmer for 10 minutes.
Add the chopped nettles and cook for another 10 minutes. Add pepper and puree.

9.21 Noodle casserole with plugs and peaches

Relieves fatigue, relaxes, good to fight belching, acute or chronic obstruction of the bowel, flatulence, heartburn. Calms nerves and stomach, strengthens the defense, good to fight fungi infections.
Cooking time approx. 1 hour
Calories p. portion: 442
4 portions
Allergens: ACGO

Quantity of ingredients:
Peaches 1,1 lbs / 500g. (yes)
Noodles (wheat, ribbon noodles) with egg 5/8 oz / 200g. (yes)
Chicken egg 2 pieces / 120g. (little)
Lemon peel 1/2 piece / 2g. ()
Vanilla sugar natural 3 package / 3g. (yes)
Cinnamon ground 1/4 teaspoon / 1g. (recommended)
Curd cheese 20% 5/8 lbs - 8oz / 250g. (recommended)
Butter Bio 2 teaspoons / 8g. (little)
Strawberry jam 4 table spoons / 50g. (yes)
Sugar - icing sugar 1/8 lbs - 2oz / 40g. (yes)

Cooking instructions:
Preheat oven to 180°C/356°F.
Put Peaches briefly in boiling water, drain and peel off the skin. Cut peaches into small slices.
Cook noodles in plenty of salted water until firm, drain, chill off cold and drain.
Separate eggs. Stir egg yolks with icing sugar, vanilla sugar, grated lemon zest and cinnamon until fluffy with the whisk. Stir in the curd cheese. Add the noodles.
Beat the egg whites into firm snow and carefully lift them under the pasta.
Spread a baking dish thinly with butter. Alternating pate noodle mixture and peach slices into the form layers. Finish with the pasta mixture.
Sprinkle the casserole with butter flakes and bake in a preheated oven for 3o minutes.
Serve portion by portion with a tablespoon of jam.

9.22 Oat Congee

Strengthens immune system.
Cooking time approx. 2-4 hours
Calories p. portion: 162
3 portions
Allergens: A

Quantity of ingredients:
Water 6 cups / 700g. (yes)
Oat 1 cup / 125g. (yes)

Cooking instructions:
Cook oats and water in a ratio of about 1: 6. The amount of water
determines the thickness of the mash (purematter of taste). The oats
swell, so do not take much. Put the oats in a saucepan with good
insulation and a heavy
lid. It is important to simmer the oats after a short boil on the slightest
flame, otherwise it burns. Cook the oat for 2-4 hours. The longer it
cooks, the more he strengthens.

9.23 Polenta with peach

Relieves fatigue, forcing spleen, diuretic, strengthens the defense, good
to fight fungi infections, lets urine and bile juice flow, prevents the aging
process, strengthens brain cells.
Cooking time approx. 20 min
Calories p. portion: 197
3 portions
Allergens:

Quantity of ingredients:
Corn Grease (Polenta) 1 cup / 120g. (yes)
Water 1 1/2 cups / 240g. (yes)
Peaches 2-3 pieces / 400g. (yes)
Vanilla pod 1 pinch / 1g. (yes)
Cinnamon ground 1 pinch / 1g. (recommended)

Cooking instructions:
Pour the polenta into a pan of hot water with constant stirring until the
polenta has the desired consistency. Pull the polenta from the fire and
let it soak for 10 minutes.

Wash fresh peaches and cut into quarters. Pour into the finished

polenta the peaches, add the vanilla and add Chili to taste, stir and let it go for 3 minutes.
Winter varieties: Pickled fruit, pear, apples

9.24 Pumpkin-yoghurt soup

Relaxes, reduces blood pressure, strengthens immune system, promotes weight loss. Good to fight immunodeficiency, loss of appetite, flatulence, depressions, diabetes, diarrhea.
Cooking time approx. 15 min
Calories p. portion: 68
4 portions
Allergens: GL

Quantity of ingredients:
Peppermint 2 leaves / 1g. ()
Basic recipe for a vegetable soup (nutritious) 1 cup / 300g. (recommended)
Anise (Common Fennel) 1/4 teaspoon / 1g. (recommended)
Salt 1 pinch / 1g. (little)
Yogurt (natural, 1.5% fat) 3/8 lbs - 6oz / 150g. (recommended)
Hokkaido pumpkin 1,1 lbs / 500g. (recommended)
Ginger fresh 1/2 teaspoon / 2g. (recommended)
Fennel seeds ground 1/2 teaspoon / 1g. (recommended)

Cooking instructions:
Heat the vegetable broth (after the basic recipe) till it boils. Add diced pumpkin, chopped ginger, crushed fennel seeds and anise. Bring the soup to the boil and simmer for about 12 minutes until the pumpkin is soft.
Remove soup from the heat. Puree the soup with the yoghurt with the blender. Serve soup with finely chopped mint sprinkled.

9.25 Puréed banana

Eat 2 times a day, regulates gastrointestinal function
Cooking time approx. 7 min
Calories p. portion: 144
1 portions
Allergens:

Quantity of ingredients:
Banana 1 piece / 150g. (yes)

Cooking instructions:
Mix the banana with the fork or purée with a blender. Leave to brown for at least 5 minutes.

9.26 Rhubarb and apple jelly

Antioxidants, lots of vitamin C, laxative, relieves pain, detoxifying, warms stomach and spleen, improves blood circulation.
Cooking time approx. 15 min
Calories p. portion: 180
2 portions
Allergens:

Quantity of ingredients:
Peppermint 2 leaves / 2g. ()
Cinnamon ground 1 pinch / 0,5g. (recommended)
Rhubarb 5/8 oz / 200g. (recommended)
Apple juice (natural cloudy) 1 cup / 300g. (yes)
Corn starch 1 oz / 30g. (yes)
Vanilla sugar natural 1 pinch / 0,5g. (yes)
Honey 1/2 oz / 20g. (recommended)

Cooking instructions:
Add the cornstarch to a 1/2 cup apple juice.
Simmer the rhubarb in 1 cup of water for 10 min.
Add the remaining apple juice and the cornstarch, stir, heat till it boils again.
Sweet with honey and season with vanilla and cinnamon. Spread the mixture on dessert bowls and garnish with mint.

9.27 Rice congee with carrots and fennel

Worms, forcing spleen, relieves constipation, stimulates nerves, detoxifying, reduces inflammation, improves blood circulation, reduces blood pressure, strengthens immune system, prevents cancer, reduces radiation
Cooking time approx. 2 hours and more
Calories p. portion: 131
3 portions
Allergens: G

Quantity of ingredients:
Basic recipe for a rice soup (Congee) 2 cup / 500g. (recommended)
Carrot 2 pieces / 100g. (recommended)
Cardamom 1/2 teaspoon / 1g. (recommended)
Fennel 1 piece / 250g. (recommended)
Butter Bio 1 teaspoon / 3g. (little)

Cooking instructions:
Cook rice congee according to basic recipe.
Clean and cut carrots and fennel.

Note:
When carrots and fennel are cooked from the beginning, they serve wholesomeness. If added shortly before the end of the cooking time, taste and vitamins are retained.

Refine with butter and cardamom before serving.

9.28 Rice with parsnips

Rich in vitamins, minerals potassium and zinc. Good to fight blood circulation disorders, thrombose, risk of embolism, high blood pressure, a headache, heart attack and stroke, yeast infections.
Cooking time approx. 45 min
Calories p. portion: 206
3 portions
Allergens:

Quantity of ingredients:
Rice variety any 1 cup / 120g. (yes)
Sage 1 teaspoon / 3g. (recommended)
Water 1 1/2 cups / 200g. (yes)
Olive oil 1 table spoon / 10g. (little)
Parsnip 3-4 pieces / 450g. (recommended)
Salt 1 pinch / 1g. (little)

Cooking instructions:
Peel the parsnips and cut into slices. Fry for a short time in oil. Add the rice and fry again for a short time. Add the water and cook it at least 30 min. Sprinkle with fresh chopped sage.

9.29 Roasted millet with Celery sticks

Promotes spleen and kidney, diuretic, promoting metabolism.
Cooking time approx. 30 min
Calories p. portion: 400
2 portions
Allergens: L

Quantity of ingredients:
Salt 1 pinch / 1g. (little)
Celery sticks 2 rods / 50g. (recommended)
Water 1 1/2 cups / 240g. (yes)
Sage 3-4 leaves / 2g. (recommended)
Millet 1 cup / 120g. (yes)
Cress 1 teaspoon / 3g. (recommended)
Water 2 table spoons / 30g. (yes)
Herbs various 1 table spoon / 10g. (yes)

Cooking instructions:
Roast millet briefly, pour over water, heat till it boils and let stand for 20 min. to swell.

Cut celery into small pieces and mix with water, salt and fresh herbs and cook for 10 min. Add to the millet.
Sprinkle fresh sage or watercress over it.

9.30 Rosemary Potatoes

Reduces Inflammation, improves digestion, regenerates skin, supports urination, lowers cholesterol. Rosemary stimulates digestion, strengthens lung, promotes spleen and kidney, dries out.
Cooking time approx. 30 min
Calories p. portion: 188
2 portions
Allergens:

Quantity of ingredients:
Salt (herbal) 1 pinch / 1g. (little)
Rosemary 1 teaspoon / 2g. (yes)
Olive oil 1 table spoon / 10g. (little)
Potato 6-8 pieces / 420g. (recommended)

Cooking instructions:
Cut the potatoes into halfs, apply a little olive oil on the cut surface, then salt, sprinkle 2 - 3 rosemary needles on the potatoes.
Place the potatoes on the baking tray and bake them in the preheated oven for approx. 25 minutes to 190°C/374°F.

9.31 Semolina soup with vegetables

Reduces blood pressure, strengthens immune system, prevents cancer, forcing spleen, dissolves stagnation, promotes weight loss. Good to fight immunodeficiency, loss of appetite, flatulence, high blood pressure, depressions, diabetes, diarrhea, rheumatism, heartburn, twelffinger intestinal ulcers.
Cooking time approx. 20 min
Calories p. portion: 105
3 portions
Allergens: AGL

Quantity of ingredients:
Cream, sweet 30% 2 table spoons / 30g. ()
Celery root 1/8 lbs - 2oz / 50g. (recommended)
Carrot 1/4 lbs - 4oz / 100g. (recommended)
Parsley 1 table spoon / 10g. (recommended)
Lovage 1/2 teaspoon / 2g. (recommended)
Wheat semolina 2 table spoons / 20g. (yes)
Basil (fresh) 1/2 teaspoon / 1g. (recommended)
Nutmeg 1 pinch / 0,1g. (recommended)
Basic recipe for a vegetable soup (nutritious) 2 cup / 500g. (recommended)

Cooking instructions:
Roast wheat grits without fat in a pan. Roast the chopped carrots and celery briefly. Add the vegetable soup (Basic recipe for a vegetable soup). Season with lovage, nutmeg and let it 10 min. simmer.
Stir in the cream before serving and garnish with parsley.

9.32 Strawberry soup with melons

Relieves pain and inflammation in rheumatism. Diuretic, helps to fight constipation.
Cooking time approx. 5 min
Calories p. portion: 87
2 portions
Allergens:

Quantity of ingredients:
Cantaloupe 5/8 oz / 200g. (recommended)
Strawberries 3/4 lbs / 300g. (recommended)
Strawberry Juice 1/3 cup / 70g. (yes)
Lemon peel 1/4 teaspoon / 1g. ()

Cooking instructions:
Puree strawberries (fresh or frozen) and strawberry juice with the blender, mix in a little sugar.
Cut melon pulp into small pieces.
Arrange strawberry soup in portions. Put the melon cubes in the sweet soup.

9.33 Tea Black tea (Russian tea)

Black tea improves blood circulation.
Cooking time approx. 10 min
Calories p. portion: 7
1 portions
Allergens:

Quantity of ingredients:
Water 1 cup / 120g. (yes)
Black tea 1 table spoon / 5g. (yes)

Cooking instructions:
For each cup you use a teaspoonful or a teabag.
Pour green tea only with 60 to 80 ° C / 140 to 176 °F hot water, otherwise it will be bitter.
If the tea has a stimulating effect, let it draw for two to three minutes. It has a calming effect for a duration of five minutes (no longer, otherwise it will be bitter!).
Another method: Pour the tea leaves with about 70 ° C / 158 °F hot water and pour the water immediately again.
Then just pour hot water again. The bitter substances disappear and the tea gets a milder aroma.

9.34 Tea from ginger with honey

Honey relieves pain, detoxifying, bactericide.
Fresh ginger encourages digestion, detoxifying, strengthens bodily production, promotes perspiration, reduces blood lipids, stimulates, dissolves stagnation.

Cooking time approx. 30 min
Calories p. portion: 5
4 portions
Allergens:

Quantity of ingredients:
Water 2 cup / 500g. (yes)
Ginger fresh 1 teaspoon / 3g. (recommended)
Honey 2 teaspoons / 6g. (recommended)

Cooking instructions:
Heat the water till it boils and put it aside. Add ginger and 20-30 min. to let go. Sweet to taste with honey.

9.35 Tea Green tea

Green tea promotes digestion, supports urination, dissolves mucus, detoxifying, stimulates nerves, reduces blood lipids, lowers cholesterol, reduces inflammation.
Cooking time approx. 10 min
Calories p. portion: 2
1 portions
Allergens:

Quantity of ingredients:
Green tea 1 teaspoon / 2g. (recommended)
Water 1 cup / 120g. (yes)

Cooking instructions:
For each cup you use a teaspoonful or a teabag.
Pour green tea only with 60 to 80 ° C / 140 to 176 °F hot water, otherwise it will be bitter.
If the tea has a stimulating effect, let it draw for two to three minutes. It has a calming effect for a duration of five minutes (no longer, otherwise it will be bitter!).
Another method: Pour the tea leaves with about 70 ° C / 158 °F hot water and pour the water immediately again.
Then just pour hot water again. The bitter substances disappear and the tea gets a milder aroma.

9.36 Tea mixture against general exhaustion

Good to fight general exhaustion. Antibacterial, encouragingly, good to fight loss of appetite, flatulence, heartburn.
Cooking time approx. 10 min
Calories p. portion: 2
4 portions
Allergens:

Quantity of ingredients:
Water 1 1/2 cups / 500g. (yes)
Lavender blossoms 1 teaspoon / 2g. (yes)
Blackberry leaves 2 teaspoons / 3g. (yes)
Lemon Balm (dried) 2 teaspoons / 3g. (yes)

Cooking instructions:
Heat the water till it boils and put it aside. Add 2 g lemon balm, 2 g blackberry leaves, 1,5g lavender flowers, leave to stand covered for 10 minutes, then strain. Drink a cup three times a day.

9.37 Vegetable potato and meat mash

Strengthens immune system, reduces inflammation, improves digestion, strengthens spleen and stomach, strengthens the muscles, tendons and bones, antiparasitic.
Cooking time approx. 30 min
Calories p. portion: 127
2 portions
Allergens:

Quantity of ingredients:
Beef meat (calf) 1/8 lbs - 2oz / 40g. (yes)
Carrot (Early Carrot) 5/8 oz / 200g. (recommended)
Potato 1/4 lbs - 4oz / 100g. (recommended)
Apricots juice 6 table spoons / 60g. (little)
Rapeseed oil 1 table spoon / 6g. (little)

Cooking instructions:
Remove the flesh, skin, tendons and grease, wash under cool water and cut into small pieces and boil in a little water. After about 15-20 minutes, remove and puree. Wash the vegetables and potatoes, peel and cut into not too small pieces. Cook gently with a little water over a low heat for 10-20 minutes. Use the blender to chop the vegetables. Mix everything, add butter or oil and fruit juice and puree again.

Alternately use other meats such as chicken, lamb or turkey. Also change vegetables with zucchini, kohlrabi, fennel, pumpkin, parsnips and broccoli.

Also change the fruit juices. This can produce a variety of flavors.

9.38 Vitamin drink

Regulates gastrointestinal function, promotes spleen and liver, reduces blood pressure, strengthens immune system, prevents cancer, reduces radiation damage, supports urination, quenches thirst, calms the stomach,
Cooking time approx. 5 min
Calories p. portion: 172
3 portions
Allergens:

Quantity of ingredients:
Orange juice 1 cup / 300g. (yes)
Carrot 5/8 oz / 200g. (recommended)
Banana 2 pieces / 300g. (yes)
Kiwi 1 piece / 20g. (yes)

Cooking instructions:
Chop oranges, carrots, bananas and kiwi and finely puree with the blender.

9.39 Zucchini semolina cream soup

Good to fight loss of appetite, reduces blood pressure, promotes weight loss. Good to fight loss of appetite, flatulence, inflammatory bowel disease, rheumatism, heartburn.
Cooking time approx. 25 min
Calories p. portion: 146
4 portions
Allergens: AGL

Quantity of ingredients:
Wheat semolina 2 table spoons / 20g. (yes)
Parsley 1 Bunch / 100g. (recommended)
Basic recipe for a vegetable soup (nutritious) 3 1/2 cups / 800g. (recommended)
Zucchini 7/8 lbs / 400g. (recommended)

Anise (Common Fennel) 1 pinch / 0,5g. (recommended)
Pepper (ground) 1 pinch / 0,5g. (little)
Lovage 1/2 teaspoon / 2g. (recommended)
Salt 1 pinch / 1g. (little)
Lemon peel 1/4 piece / 2g. ()
Crème fraiche cheese 2 table spoons / 20g. ()
Butter Bio 1/2 oz / 20g. (little)
Ginger fresh 1/2 teaspoon / 1g. (recommended)
Nutmeg 1 pinch / 0,5g. (recommended)

Cooking instructions:
Melt the butter in a saucepan, add the semolina and fry briefly while stirring. Add half of the chopped parsley, sauté for a short time, pour vegetable broth according to the basic recipe, season with chopped lovage, nutmeg and anise. Cook the soup without lid lightly for 10 minutes. Add the finely chopped zucchini and the small piece of lemon zest, cook gently for 5 minutes until the zucchini are tender. Remove the lemon peel.
Using the blender, finely puree the soup with the crème fraiche and the remaining parsley.

10 Effects of food

10.1 Use ingredients: recommendable

Acai powder
Anise (Common Fennel)
Apple puree
Artichoke
Asparagus (green or white)
Aubergine
Basic recipe for a beef soup
Basic recipe for a beef soup (warming)
Basic recipe for a chicken soup (warming)
Basic recipe for a fish soup
Basic recipe for a rice soup (Congee)
Basic recipe for a vegetable soup (nutritious)
Basil
Basil (fresh)
Bay leaf
Bearberry leaf
Beef fillet
Beef meatbones
Bitter Herb liqueur
Black caraway
Blackberry´s
Blue mallow tee
Blueberry
Blueberry dried
Borage
Bread roll
Bread with carob kernel flour
Buckwheat
Bulgur (cereals)
Cantaloupe
Cardamom
Carrot
Carrot (Early Carrot)
Carrot juice without sugar
Celery root
Celery sticks
Chamomile tea
Channa-Dal
Chard
Chenpi (chinese tangerine bowl)
Chicken meat
Chinese pearl barley
Chlorella (fresh water)
Cinnamon ground
Cinnamon sticks
Clove
Cod

Codfish
Coix (seeds) YiYi Ren
Compote (fruits of the season)
Coriander
Cottage cheese
Cow's milk (1.5% fat)
Cranberry
Cranberry juice
Cream 10% coffee cream
Cress
Crucian
Curd cheese 20%
Currant (black)
Currant (red)
Currant (white)
Dandelion (young plants)
Dandelionroots tea
Deer meat
Deer meat
Dill
Dyer's broom herb
Elderberries
Elderberry blossom tee
Evening primrose oil
Fennel
Fennel seeds ground
Fennel tea
Fish pieces mixed (fresh water)
Fox nut, gorgon nut, makhana
Fructose (glucose)
Gail plum
Galangal
Gelee Royal
Gentian root tea
Ginger fresh
Ginseng
Gooseberry
Gourd
Grass carp
Green tea
Ground
Ground caraway
Guava
Hibiscus
Hokkaido pumpkin
Honey
Juniper berry
Kombu seaweed (Saccharina japonica)
Kudzu

Kukicha tea
Ladyfingers
Lamb's lettuce
Lamb's lettuce
Lily bulbs
Loquate / Japanese medlar
Lotus roots
Lotus seeds
Lovage
Luo Han Guo fruit
Mascarpone cheese
Miso black (fermented)
Mu Erh Mushroom
Nori, purple seaweed, red algae
Nutmeg
Orange blossom
Oregano dried
Oregano fresh
Parsley
Parsnip
Pearl barley
Perch
Pheasant
Plaice
Potato
Potato (mealy)
Prickly pear
Processed cheese 12%
Pumpkin
Quail
Rabbit
Rabbit (wild)
Rabbit meat
Radicchio
Raspberry

Red beet
Rhubarb
Rice noodles
Rose hip
Rose hip tea
Rosefish
Rucola
Safflower (Dyer's thistle / Hong Hua)
Sage
Salsify
Sea cucumber
Shark
Sour milk cheese 20%
Spelled flakes
Spelled semolina
St. Benedict's thistle, blessed thistle, holy thistle, spotted thistle
Strawberries
Sweet potato
Topinambur
Turkey breast meat
Turnip
Turnips
Vegetable juice
Wakame
Watermelon
Wax gourd
Whey
Wild boar meat
Wild herbs
Yew nut
Yoghurt vanilla
Yogurt (natural, 1.5% fat)
Zucchini

10.2 Use ingredients: yes

Acerola fruit nectar or powder
Agar agar (kelp)
Agave nectar
Agrimony
Aloe juice
Amaranth
Amaranth Pops
Angelica root
Apple (sour)
Apple (sweet)
Apple juice (natural cloudy)
Apricot
Apricot jam
Apricot nectar
Arrowroot
Baking powder

Balm
Bamboo shoots
Banana
Banana (cooking banana)
Banchatee (green tea)
barberry
Barley
Barley flour
Barley grass powder
Barley grouts
Barley malt
Barley not peeled
Batavia
Beef heart (calf)
Beef meat
Beef meat (calf)

Beef Oxtail pieces
Beef soup meat
Berries of the season
Berry juice
Bitter Lemon
Bitter orange peel
Black tea
Blackberry dried (unripe fruit)
Blackberry jam
Blackberry leaves
Blackthorn (Sloe)
Blueberry jam
Blueberry juice
Bocksdorn fruits (Fructus Lycii, Goji, goji berry dried
Breadcrumbs (wheat bread, bread roll)
Broccoli
Buckbean
Burdock root tea
Buttermilk
Calamari
Capers in olive oil
Carambola (Star fruit)
Carob flour, St. john's bread
Caviar
Cereal coffee
Chamomile
Chervil
Chervil dried
Chicken egg white
Chicory
Chrysanthemum blossom tea
Clarified butter
Clementine
Cocoa
Coriander (fresh)
Corn
Corn (fast polenta)
Corn flour
Corn Grease (Polenta)
Corn silk tea
Corn starch
Couscous
Cow's milk (whole milk 3.5% fat)
Crab
Cranberries
Cranberry
Cranberry jam
Creamer
Crispbread
Cumin (Caraway seed)
Curcuma
Currant jam (black)
Currant jam (red)

Currant juice (black)
Daisy
Dandelion juice
Dashi
Dates red
Deer's Bones
Dulse (seaweed)
Endive salad
Fenugreek (Trigonella foenum-graecum)
Feta cheese
Fig
Fish sauce
Flounder
Flower pollen
Freshwater crab
Freshwater fish
Fruit mix juice
Fruit tea
Gelatin white
Gentian root
Ginger powder
Ginkgo fruit
Ginseng root
Goat
Goat and sheep's milk
Goat cheese
Grape juice red
Grape juice white
Green spelt
Halibut (Flatfish)
Hawthorn
Herbs bitter
Herbs of Provence
Herbs various
Herbs wild
Hibiscus tea
Hijiki
Horehound leaves
Horse meat
Hyssop
Iceberg lettuce
Jasmine blossoms tee
Jellyfish
Kaki plum
Kalmus
Kefir
King Solomon's-seal
Kiwi
Kumquats
Lamb bones
Lamb meat
Lamb shoulder
Lavender blossoms

Leaf salads (bitter)
Lemon Balm (dried)
Lemon Balm (fresh)
Lemongrass
Lettuce
Licorice root tea
Lime blossom tea
Liver smoothing tea
Lobster
Longane
Lovage seeds
Lychee
Lye roll
Mallow (Malva sylvestris) blossom tea
Malt
Mango
Mango juice
Mare's milk
Margarine
Margarine (diet)
Marjoram
Mediterranean fish (cod, plaice, haddock, sea eel, mackerel)
Medlar
Millet
Millet flakes
Miso
Miso paste (soy bean paste)
Mulberry fruit
Mulled Wine Spice
Mullet
Mussels
Mustard seeds
Mutton
Nasturtium (nose-twister or nose-tweaker)
Nectarine
Nettles
Noodles (wheat) with egg
Noodles (wheat, lasagne) with egg
Noodles (wheat, ribbon noodles) with egg
Noodles (wheat, spaghetti) with egg
Oat
Oat flakes roasted
Oat flour
Oat meal
Oat milk
Octopus
Octopus
Okra
Orange
Orange jam
Orange juice

Papaya
Parsley root
Passion blossoms tea
Passion fruit
Peaches
Peaches (canned)
Pear juice
Pearl barley
Pigeon
Pimento
Pineapple
Pineapple juice without sugar
Pomegranate
Pork ham
Pork ham cooked
Pork ham smoked
Pork knuckle
Pork marrow bones
Potato flour
Pudding powder vanilla
Quince
Quinoa
Radish
Radish leaves
Raspberry dried (immature)
Raspberry jam
Raspberry leaf tea
Red berry (without sugar)
Ribworttea
Rice (fragrance)
Rice (Gaoliang / Sorghum)
Rice Basmati
Rice flour
Rice long grain rice
Rice malt
Rice round grain
Rice starch
Rice sticky
Rice sweet
Rice variety any
Romaine lettuce / lettuce salad
Rose blossom tea
Rose leaf tea
Rosemary
Rusk
Rye flour
Saffron
Sago (cereals)
Sea buckthorn
Seacrab
Sheep's milk
Sheep's milk yoghurt
Shrimp
Shrimps

Skim milk powder
Slug
Sorrel
Sourdough
Soy sauce
Soy Tofu
Spelled (Dark) bread
Spelled grain
Spelled wholemeal flour
Spinach
Spiny lobsters
Spurdog (spiny dogfish, Schillerlocken)
Star anise
Stevia (candyleaf, sweetleaf)
Strawberry jam
Strawberry Juice
Sugar - icing sugar
Sugar brown
Sugar candy white
Sugar cane sugar
Sugar fructose - fruit sugar
Sugar glucose - grapes sugar
Sugar Milk Sugar
Sugar molasses
Sugar palm sugar
Sugar substitute (sweetener)
Sugar white
Supplementary nutrition
Tangerine
Tarragon (Estragon)
Tea mixture uric acid lowering
Thyme
Thyme dried
Tomato
Tomato juice
Tomato paste
Tomato puree
Tonic Water

Trout
Tsampa (roasted barley flour)
Turkey ham
Turmeric (yellow root)
Umeboshi paste
Valerian
Vanilla
Vanilla pod
Vanilla powder
Vanilla sugar natural
Water
Water hot
Wheat
Wheat bulgur
Wheat flakes
Wheat flatbread/pita bread
Wheat flour
Wheat semolina
Wheat semolina for children
Wheatgrass juice
Wheatgrass powder
White bread (baguette)
White bread (pretzel sticks)
White bread (roll)
White bread (wheat bread)
White breadcrumbs
White dumpling bread (wheat bread cut into chunks)
Whitefish
Wild garlic (garlic spinach)
Wild strawberries
Wormwood herb
Yam root, yam root tuber
Yarrow
Yarrow tea
Yogi tea
Yogurt (natural, 3.5% fat)

10.3 Use ingredients: little

Apricot dried
Apricots juice
Avocado
Buckwheat (roasted) Kasha
Buckwheat whole grain
Butter (half fat)
Butter Bio
Cauliflower
Cherry compote
Cherry juice
Chestnut puree
Chestnuts

Chicken egg
Chicken yolk
Coconut flakes
Coconut grated
Coconut meat
Coconut milk
Corn (roasted)
Corn germ oil
Cream sour 10%
Currants (black)
Currants (red)
Curry

Dates dried
Ducks egg
Edam cheese
Fig dried
Fresh cheese
Fresh cheese from soya
Fresh cheese with herbs
Garam Masala powder
Goose egg
Gouda cheese
Grapes red
Grapes white
Grapeseed oil
Herbal tea mix
Kohlrabi
Linseed oil
Lychee in Preserved
Manioc flour
Mineral water
Mold cheese
Mozzarella
Muesli
Multi-grain bread (gray bread)
Mung bean sprouting
Mustard
Mustard Dijon
Mustard medium hot
Mustard sweet
Mutton
Noodles (whole grain) with egg
Olive oil
Oyster mushroom
Oyster shell powder
Oysters
Pear
Pepper (ground)
Pepper white (ground)
Peppercorns
Pigeon egg
Pineapple (from a can)
Poppy

Pork meat
Pumpkin seed oil
Quail egg
Radish (white, green, purple-red)
Radish black
Raisins
Rapeseed oil
Rice (whole grain)
Rice black
Rice mash
Rice red
Rice wild (nature rice)
Sake
Salmon
Salt
Salt (herbal)
Sesame oil
Sesame oil roasted
Sesame, black
Sesame, white
Sour cream 15% fat
Sour milk
Soy flour
Soy noodles
Soybean milk
Soybean oil
Sunflower oil
Sunflower seeds
Toast bread (whole grain)
Tomato dried
Tuna
Vinegar (Apple vinegar)
Vinegar (Red wine vinegar)
Vinegar Aceto Balsamico
Vinegar Aceto Balsamico white
Walnut oil
Wheat flour whole grain
Wheat germ oil
Wheat/Rye/Gray-black bread with yeast
Wholemeal flour
Yeast

10.4 Do not use contra-acting foods

Adzuki beans
Almond
Almond marzipan
Almond milk
Almond puree
Anchovy / Sardine
Apricots
Basic recipe for a duck soup
Bean oil
Beans (green, fresh)

Beef bone marrow
Beef heart
Beef kidney
Beef liver
Beef lungs (calf)
Beef stomach
Beer (alcohol-free)
Beer (alcohol-reduced)
Beer (Pils)
Beer (Top-fermented German dark

beer)
Bitter liqueur
Black beans
Black fungus mushroom
Black-eyed peas
Boletus mushroom
Borage oil
Boxhorn clover seeds
Brazil nuts
Brie cheese
Broad beans (thick beans)
Brown ale
Brussels sprouts
Bush beans
Butter beans white
Camembert
Campari
Carp
Cashews
Champignon
Chanterelle
Cherry
Cherry (sour)
Chicken Blood
Chicken heart
Chicken liver
Chicken stomach
Chickpeas
Chickweed
Chili (pod or ground)
Chinese cabbage
Chives
Chocolate
Chocolate (Diabetic)
Clementines
Coconut fat
Coffee
Cola drink
Cola drink (low calorie)
Cooking oil
Cream (30% fat)
Cream sour 20%
Cream sour 30%
Cream, sweet 30%
Crème fraiche cheese
Cucumber
Cucumber (bitter)
Cucumber (spicy cucumber)
Curd cheese 40%
Curry paste red
Deer's kidneys
Duck (heart)
Duck (slaughtered)
Eel

Eel smoked
Emmental cheese
Fernet Branca (herbal bitter liqueur)
Feta cheese
Fish innards
Fish remains
French beans
Garlic
Ginger oil
Ginseng liqueur
Goat and sheep's blood
Goat and sheep's brain
Goat and sheep's liver
Goat and sheep's stomach
Goose
Goose blood
Goose fat
Goose parts
Gorgonzola
Grapefruit (Pomelo)
Grapefruit dried peel
Grapefruit juice
Greengage
Hazelnuts
Herring
Honey wine (Met)
Hop
Kidney beans (red)
Lamb kidneys
Lamb liver
Leek
Lemon
Lemon juice
Lemon peel
Lentils
Lentils black
Lentils red
Lentils yellow
Lima beans
Lime
Linseed
Linseed (crushed)
Lychee liqueur
Mackerel
Maple syrup
Martini
Mayonnaise 50%
Mayonnaise 80%
Mirabelle plum
Mixed Pickles
Morel (black, dried)
Morel, dried
Mung bean
Oat flakes (whole grain)

Oat fusion (baby food)
Olives
Olives green
Onion (shallot)
Onion (spring onion)
Onion read
Onion white
Orange dried peel
Orange grated peel
Orange peel
Palm oil
Parmesan
Peanut (roasted)
Peanut butter
Peanut oil
Peanuts
Peas
Peas, green
Pepper Cayenne
Pepper powder (hot)
Peppermint
Peppermint tea
Pepperoni
Pepperoni, red, pitted, halved
Pepperoni, yellow, pitted, halved
Peppers
Peppers (rose peppers)
Peppers (sweet)
Peppers powder
Pickle
Pig blood
Pine nuts
Pinto beans speckled
Pistachios
Plum
Plum dried
Plums
Pork Bacon
Pork brain
Pork fat (lard)
Pork heart
Pork kidneys
Pork Lard
Pork liver
Pork lung
Pork sausage (Bratwurst)
Pork skin

Pork stomach
Pork/beef sausage (smoked)
Pork's intestine
Processed cheese 30%
Prosecco
Psyllium seed
Puff pastry
Pumpernickel (dark bread)
Pumpkin seeds
Rabbit liver
Radish horseradish
Red cabbage
Contraindicated food
Red wine
Reishi mushroom
Rum
Rye
Rye wholemeal bread
Sauerkraut (cutted cabbage fermented)
Savory
Savoy cabbage / kale
Sesame paste (Tahini)
Sherry (whine)
Shiitake, dried
Sour cherries
Soy Tofu smoked
Soya Cuisine (soy cream)
Soybeans
Soybeans, black
Soybeans, blacks, fermented
Soybeans, yellow
Spirit
Tabasco
Thistle oil
Trout (smoked)
Truffle
Umeboshi plums (Japanese apricots)
Walnuts
Walnuts roasted
Wheat beer
Wheat bran
White beans
White cabbage
White wine
Whole grain bread
Wormwood

11 Herbs and their effects

11.1 Basil (fresh)

It has a beneficial effect on flatulence and nausea, relaxing and soothing. Good to fight emphysema, bronchitis, whooping cough, high blood pressure, headache, mouth odor, warts, hiccup, gout, migraine.

11.2 Nettles

Promotes urination. Tea or juice, cleanses the blood and the kidneys, supports prostate problems, inhibit the formation of inflammation, pain-relieving.

11.3 Blackberry leaves

Good to fight diarrhea, inflammation of the mucous membrane of the mouth, make mouth rinse.

11.4 Herbs various

Appetizing, lots of trace elements and vitamins

11.5 Cress

Diuretic, supports urination. Good to fight dry mouth, inner agitation, sore throat, diabetes, kidney stones, gastrointestinal complaints, lung problems, menstrual cramps or cancer.

11.6 Lavender blossoms

Calms the central nervous system, relieves anxiety, to fight sleep disturbances, loss of appetite and nervous intestinal complaints.

11.7 Lovage

Stimulates digestion, reduces pain. Extracts of the root are used to flush out urinary tract infections and prevent kidney gravel.

11.8 Parsley

Stimulates liver function, detoxifies. Forces urinating. Relieves flatulence. Digestive and menstrual stimulating, birth-accelerating, memory-enhancing, blood-purifying, skin-smoothing.

11.9 Peppermint

Relaxes, frees the lungs and the nose (inhale), regulates the cycle. Stimulates bile flow and bile production, antispasmodic in gastrointestinal disorders, antimicrobial and antiviral.

11.10   Rosemary

Promotes digestion, relieves bloating, strengthens lung, spleen and kidney. Affects the circulation and nerves. Appetizing. Baths help to fight circulatory disorders as well as with gout and rheumatism.

11.11   Sage

Good to fight yeast infections. The leaves have a digestive effect and are used in greasy foods. Antiperspirant effect. Helps to relieve coughing attacks. Dries out (TCM).

11.12   Thyme dried

Disinfecting. It stimulates the blood circulation, increases the appetite and helps to digest fat meat better. Strengthens lungs and spleen (TCM).

11.13   Lemon Balm (fresh)

Stimulating, antibacterial, encouraging, relaxing, antispasmodic, cooling, antipyretic, analgesic, sweat-inducing, virus-inhibiting. Good for colds, fever, flu, cough, bronchitis, asthma, loss of appetite, bloating, heartburn.

11.14   Lemon Balm (dried)

Stimulating, antibacterial, encouraging, relaxing, antispasmodic, cooling, antipyretic, analgesic, sweat-inducing, virus-inhibiting. Good for colds, fever, flu, cough, bronchitis, asthma, loss of appetite, bloating, heartburn.

12 Basics of Nutrition

The basic principles of nutrition described herein are general recommendations. They are not aimed at a specific form of therapy. Recommendations concerning a therapy have priority.

12.1 Nutrition

Regular meals in a relaxed atmosphere. A warm breakfast is considered a good start into the day.

The main meals ought to be taken for lunch – supper in the early evening. Pay attention to feeling hungry or sated: don't eat too much nor remain hungry is the rule

Prepare the meals freshly from natural, regional products. Frozen, heat-conserved, industrially prepared or foodstuffs cooked in the microwave oven are rejected.

Choice of foodstuffs according to the season: more cooling food in summer, more warming food in winter.

Eat cooked food at least twice a day. Food and drinks ought to be lukewarm, never ice-cold or hot.

Raw vegetables, briefly cooked vegetables, freshly squeezed juices and mineral water are not recommended. Milk and dairy products are only included in the diet if they don't cause problems.

Don't use therapeutic recipes over a longer period without consulting your doctor or therapist.

Varied food
Enjoy the diversity of foodstuffs. Characteristics of a balanced nutrition are variety, suitable combination and a balanced quantity of rich and low energy foodstuffs (on one hand avoiding undersupply with essential nutrients and on the other hand to take to many undesirable substances).

A lot of Cereal Products - and Potatoes
Bread, pasta, rice, cereal flakes (best wholemeal) as well as potatoes contain almost no fat, but many vitamins, mineral nutrients, trace elements, roughage and secondary plant substances. These foodstuffs ought to be taken with low-fat side dishes.

Vegetables and Fruit – „Take Five" every day …
5 portions of vegetables and fruit a day, as fresh as possible, briefly cooked, or maybe one portion as a juice – ideal as a side dish to every meal as well as snack between meals: Thus a lot of vitamins, mineral nutrients as well as roughage and secondary plant substances

Daily milk and dairy products
Milk and Dairy Products every Day, once or twice per Week Fish;
meat, sausages as well as eggs moderately. These foodstuffs contain
valuable nutrients like calcium in the milk, iodine selenium and omega-3
fat acids in saltwater fish. Meat is favorable due to its high content of
disposable iron and the vitamins B1, B6 and B12. Quantities of 300 – 600
g meat and sausage per week are sufficient. Prefer low-fat products,
especially in meat- and dairy products.

Low-fat and fatty Foodstuffs
Fat supplies us with essential fat acids and fatty foodstuffs contain also
fat-soluble vitamins. Fat is high in energy; therefore much fat in the food
may cause overweight, possibly also cancer. Too many saturated fat
acids may further a tendency for cardio-vascular diseases in the long
term. Prefer vegetable oils and fats (e.g. rapeseed-, olive-, soya-oils and
solid fats produced therefrom). Beware of invisible fat in meat- and dairy
products, pastry and sweets as well as in fast-food and convenience
foods. 70 – 90 g fat per day is sufficient.

Moderately Sugar and Salt
Take sugar and foods/drinks containing various kinds of sugar (e.g.
glucose syrup) only occasionally. Use herbs and spices as well as a little
salt creatively. Prefer salt containing iodine.

Plenty of Liquids
Water is absolutely essential. Drink 1-2 l liquids every day. Prefer water
(with or without gas) and other low-calorie drinks. Alcoholic drinks should
not be taken.

Tasty Dishes, carefully cooked
Cook the meals with as low temperatures and as short as possible, using
little water and fat – this preserves the original taste, keeps the nutrients
intact and prevents the production of harmful compounds.

Take time and enjoy the food
Take your Time and enjoy your Food
Eating consciously helps to eat right. The eye enjoys food, too. It's fun,
invites to enjoy varied dishes and stimulates the feeling of satiety.

Watch your Weight and stay in Motion
A balanced diet and a lot of exercise and sport (30 – 60 min/day) are a
healthy combination. The right weight furthers well-being and health.
Thermals, directional effectiveness, digestive power

There are various criteria for judging the effectiveness of herbs and foodstuffs.

The use of certain herbs and ingredients is based on observations of the effects on the body which these foodstuffs, herbs and spices show after having eaten them. The medical science has developed following system: Every ingredient or herb has a directional effectiveness. Furthermore, there are herbs which have a special effect on certain organs.

The basic condition for a healthy metabolism is to obtain sufficient energy from food and that the digestive process doesn't use too much energy. An easily digestible meal makes content and sated, doesn't cause flatulence and fatigue after the meal. The perfect spices increase the healthiness of our meals. Very often, just small doses of herbs and spices will suffice. They are not used to make us sated, but to help our digestive organs to digest the food.

12.2 Recipes

The recipes list the ingredients to be used and the cooking instructions show how the dish is prepared. The list of ingredients shows the concerned quantities as well as the relevance for the therapy. If you find „less than mentioned", try to comply or find an alternative from the „list of recommended foodstuffs". Mostly it shall result just in a small change of taste when you simply avoid this ingredient.

Mild cooking methods: boiling, stewing, poaching, steaming
Strong cooking methods: barbecuing, roasting, frying, smoking
Balanced cooking methods: deep-frying, baking brick
Deep-freezing and warming in the microwave oven should be avoided (denaturalization).

12.3 Foodstuffs

Foodstuffs have an effect on body and soul like medicinal herbs, only a very much milder one. Dietary advice is mainly based on regional foodstuffs. The knowledge about the effects of each foodstuff and the knowledge, when which foodstuff shall be used, is based on the orthodox school of medicine. Use ecologic-organic products, if possible. As everything should be cooked for a long time due to a better digestability and very rarely eaten raw, the food agrees with everyone.

The classification of the foodstuffs according to their effect on the body is the basis in order to achieve a harmonious status of health.

Dietary advisors do not recommend certain foodstuffs for everyone. The individual diet is tailor-made for the individual constitution.

Buy only fresh and ripe fruit and vegetables. You ought to leave unripe fruit and vegetables and such with brown spots and wilted leaves behind in the market. In this case take deep-frozen goods (never ready-to-serve dishes!). Fruit and vegetables are deep-frozen immediately after harvesting and often contain more vitamins and minerals than the goods from the vegetable shelf. Whereas conserved or tinned goods contain very much less biological substances. Also, salt, sugar and others are mostly added to the latter. Never leave the foodstuffs in the water after washing them to avoid that many vital substances get drowned. Clean salads, fruit and vegetables immediately before serving.

Please make sure of the hygienic processing of foodstuffs. Clean your salads, fruit and vegetables carefully. When cooking with meat, prepare all ingredients first and then process the meat products. Clean the worktop and tools very carefully. Wooden surfaces ought to be treated with a mild disinfectant regularly in order to reduce germination.

Store fruit and vegetables separately, if possible. Harvested fruit and vegetables are still alive and emit e.g. ethylene gas, which makes other products ripen and age faster. Keep meat and fish in the closed packaging or store them in the fridge in closed containers.

12.4 Herbs

There are some basic rules for storing medicinal herbs. On principle, herbs must be protected from direct sunlight, humidity and heat.

Containers for the storage of herbs may be glasses, ceramic jars and even plastic containers. However, plastic is a rather unsuitable material and should only be a short-term solution. In case of glass containers, use a dark material.

Medicinal herbs cannot be kept for any long period. The shelf life of herbs is limited. However, it can be prolonged with suitable storage. The place should be dark, rather cool and absolutely dry. A wooden medicine cabinet, placed not directly next to a source of heat, would be ideal. Never buy large quantities of herbs so as not to have to throw them away. Label the container with the name of the herb and the date of harvesting or processing.

13 Other dietic-books

The following syndromes of dietetics, TCM or for a therapy supplement for cancer are available.

Dietetics

E001. Nutrition of the infant - baby food
E002. Nutrition during lactation
E003. Nutrition in old age
E004. Nutrition of children and adolescents
E005. Nutrition of athletes
E006. Light weight
E007. Pregnancy
E008. Full food

Protein and electrolyte - kidneys
E009. (hemodialysis) dialysis treatment
E010. Acute renal failure
E011. Chronic renal insufficiency
E012. Nephrotic syndrome
E013. Kidney stones (nephrolithiasis)

Gastrointestinal tract - pancreas
E014. Acute pancreatitis (inflammation of the pancreas)
E015. Chronic pancreatitis (inflammation of the pancreas)

Gastrointestinal tract - small intestine and large intestine
E016. Acute obstipation (constipation)
E017. Chronic obstipation (constipation)
E018. Colon irritabile
E019. Diverticulitis
E020. Acquired lactose intolerance (lactose malabsorption)
E021. Fructose malabsorption
E022. Glutensensitive enteropathy (celiac disease)
E023. Colectomy
E024. Short Bowel Syndrome

Gastrointestinal tract - liver, gallbladder, bile ducts
E025. Acute and chronic hepatitis (inflammation of the liver)
E026. Cholelithiasis (bile stones)
E027. fatty liver
E028. cirrhosis

Gastrointestinal tract - Stomach and duodenal intestine
E029. Acute gastritis
E030. Chronic gastritis
E031. Stomach bleeding
E032. Ulcus ventriculi and duodenal ulcer
E033. Condition after gastric surgery

Gastrointestinal tract - oral cavity and esophagus
E034. Stomatitis
E035. Esophageal carcinoma (esophageal cancer)
E036. Refluosophagitis (heartburn)

Special diseases
E037. Phenylketonuria (PKU)
E038. Rheumatic joint diseases

Metabolism
E039. Obesity (overweight)
E040. Diabetes mellitus
E041. Eating disorders (underweight)

Fat metabolism
E042. Hypercholesterolaemia (increased cholesterol level)
E043. Hepatic Encephalopathy

Heart and circulation
E044. Arteriosclerosis (arterial calcification)
E045. Heart insufficiency
E046. Hypertension
E047. Hyperuricaemia and gout

Changed nutrient requirements
E048. In case of fever
E049. For malignant diseases
E050. After burns
E051. Radiation and chemotherapy

CANCER
E100. Pancreatic cancer
E101. Bladder cancer
E102. Blood cancer (leukemia)
E103. Breast cancer
E104. Colorectal cancer
E105. Gastric cancer
E106. Kidney cancer
E107. Esophageal cancer

TCM
E200. Bladder - moisture heat in the bladder
E201. Bladder - moisture and cold in the bladder
E202. Bladder - emptiness and cold in the bladder
E203. Large intestine - external cold affects the large intestine
E204. Large intestine - moisture heat in the large intestine
E205. Large intestine - heat blocks the intestine II acute
E206. Large intestine - dryness of the colon
E207. Large intestine - Yang deficiency (cold)
E208. Heart - Blood insufficiency
E209. Heart - Blood stagnation
E210. Heart - Fire
E211. Heart - Hot mucus clogs the heart pores

E212. Heart - Cold mucus clogs the heart pores
E213. Heart - Qi deficiency
E214. Heart - Yang deficiency
E215. Heart - Yin deficiency
E216. Liver - Ascending Liver Yang
E217. Liver - Blood deficiency
E218. Liver - Blood stagnation
E219. Liver - Moisture heat in liver and gall bladder
E220. Liver - Fire
E221. Liver - Gall bladder Qi-Empty
E222. Liver - Cold in the liver meridian
E223. Liver - Qi stagnation
E224. Liver - Wind
E225. Liver - Wind with ascending liver Yang
E226. Liver - Wind with blood anemic
E227. Liver - Wind with extreme heat
E228. Lung - Qi deficiency
E229. Lung - Mucus-moisture in the lungs
E230. Lung - Mucus-heat in the lungs
E231. Lung - Mucus-cold in the lungs
E232. Lung - Dryness of the lungs
E233. Lung - Wind-heat attacks the lungs
E234. Lung - Wind-cold affects the lungs
E235. Lung - Yin deficiency
E236. Stomach - Bloodstagnation
E237. Stomach - Fire
E238. Stomach - Cold with liquid
E239. Stomach - Nutrition stagnation
E240. Stomach - Qi deficiency
E241. Stomach - Rebellious Qi
E242. Stomach - Yin Emptiness
E243. Spleen - Heat and moisture attack the spleen
E244. Spleen - Coldness and moisture affects the spleen
E245. Spleen - Qi deficiency
E246. Spleen - Qi deficiency + Declining spleen Qi
E247. Spleen - Qi deficiency + spleen does not control the blood
E248. Spleen - Yang deficiency
E249. Kidney - Heart and kidney no longer communicate
E250. Kidney - Jing deficiency
E251. Kidney - Kidneys cannot receive the Qi
E252. Kidney - Qi is not stable
E253. Kidney - Yang deficiency
E254. Kidney - Yin deficiency

For further information visit di-book.com.